I Feel at Home

Apple Farm Celebrates Fifty Years

I Feel at Home

Apple Farm Celebrates Fifty Years

culture is not optional
Three Rivers, Michigan

First edition, October 2013

Apple Farm Community
12291 Hoffman Rd.
Three Rivers, MI 49093
www.applefarmcommunity.org

Cover design: the vg-r collective (www.vg-r.com)
Interior design: the vg-r collective (www.vg-r.com)

Published by *culture is not optional
P.O. Box 1
Three Rivers, MI 49093

For more information about *culture is not optional, visit our web site:
www.cultureisnotoptional.com

ISBN 978-0-9814839-3-1

for Helen Luke

Contents

THIS IS THE PLACE: MEMORIES OF THE FARM

THE LIVING WORD: POETRY INSPIRED BY APPLE FARM

Quotes from Jane Bishop, selected by Donald Raiche,
appear on pages 11, 46, 52, 87,

Introduction

Apple Farm was born from the vision and wisdom of Helen Luke and carried through the efforts of many over the past 50 years. In celebration of this milestone, the current board of Apple Farm extended an invitation to enter into an exploration of Helen's ideas. Responses to this invitation, which you hold collected in this commemorative book, ranged from poetry and essays, to letters and photographs.

If Helen were still writing today, her thoughts would have continued to grow and evolve. Since her death in 1996, her ideas have continued to grow and evolve in a different way in the minds and souls of all who were touched by her wisdom.

With this legacy in mind, we ask: how does Helen's work still inform us now? How does the wisdom of Apple Farm continue to live in the world and what needs to be expressed now? With the vast world of consciousness in front of us, what role does the Farm play in exploring the various territories? How have the seeds Helen helped plant matured over the years? What veins of consciousness are still opening to her presence and the wisdom of the Farm?

We invite you to enter into Helen's legacy, and the past, present and future of the Apple Farm Community.

John Howie
October 2013

50 Years of Memories, Dreams and Reflections

*ane Bishop, Else Hope, Helen Luke and Nancy Hector at Priory Farm in
November 1963.*

THE ROUND HOUSE

on Apple Farm's thirtieth anniversary

What started out as a gazebo turned into a twelve sided, thirty-foot diameter building with a beautifully raftered ceiling.

What loves, what dreams, what actions were behind these things? Who could have seen Apple Farm in their future thirty years ago? Or five years ago—or anytime? How do we know what dream remembered, written down, pondered, played with, shared with one other person, will bring to us a Round House or a painting class or a celebration or a—who knows what next?

Wherever it starts it will take each of those involved to recognize their part—to be open to a new idea, to be willing to take a risk, to take action, to welcome the coming guest in whatever guise he or she or it comes.

Jane Bishop

Apple Farm Beginnings

Janet Witt

Bud and I, with our two small boys (Carl was four years old and Ivan was two), arrived in Three Rivers in April 1963. When we came, there was no Apple Farm. There were four women—strong, courageous women knowing that they were here for something, but not knowing what, ready to accept whatever was to be.

Helen was living in Three Rivers in a small house and Else, Jane and Nancy had rented a farmhouse from St. Gregory's Abbey. People were coming to see Helen and needed a place to stay so we all started looking for property. We found the "right" place. Bud and I bought the 50 acres, kept 10 acres for ourselves and the other 40 acres became and still are the Apple Farm. Now, we could begin.

People were coming; Apple Farm was growing. The house needed much work, the land needed to be cleared, a place was needed for the few farm animals that were already part of the "family." Someone saw an old school house that could be moved onto the property for the animals. It arrived, disheveled and needing a total make over, not for the animals, but as a place for people to stay and Tali House was "born." Father Abbot asked what our "master plan" was and to this day Apple Farm is still trying to figure that out.

We all put in many long hours to get our Apple Farm in tip-top shape. As each place was fixed up, someone moved in. If we were not having work parties to fix everything up, we were having work parties to help someone move. It was exciting to see and be part of this nucleus that was becoming more and more of a community—a community unlike any we had ever heard of. There were no rules and regulations. There were no shoulds and oughts. It was a fellowship made up of people trying to be and working hard at being individuals—each one being as true to oneself as possible.

For 50 years this Apple Farm Community has been alive and growing and changing. We have had good times and we have had difficult times. We have had many crises and each one has made us stop and reevaluate and look at ourselves to find out what wants to happen. Each crisis has helped us grow individually, as well as Apple Farm itself—ever changing and still the same. I am very grateful to Helen Luke for the journey she has given me, for my Apple Farm friends and for the 50 years of support I have received from Apple Farm.

August 2013

Jane, Else, Helen and Nancy ready for Major's wedding in April 1965. Else borrowed a fancy hat for the occasion from Florence Marsh.

Building Memories

BRUCE HEUSTIS

MEETING ROBERT JOHNSON

In 1965, when I was about 16 years old, my mother, Catherine, was so enthusiastic about her inner work with Helen Luke that she proposed that my father and I go for an individual session with Robert Johnson at St. John's house. Somehow this proposal took root and my father and I dutifully got in the car and drove down to Three Rivers to meet with Robert. I have some vague memories of this event—the old farmhouse, Robert's harpsichord in the living room, a tour of the barn behind the house by one of the younger men living with Robert, a noon meal and a somewhat awkward talk with Robert—but what I remember most about this trip was the drive home when I turned to my father and asked, "What was that all about?"

A GROWING FARM CONNECTION

During my college years I began to read Helen's writings. I remember *Vow and Doctrine in the New Age* and the impression it made on me. I even wrote a paper on *The Tibetan Book of the Dead* based on Helen's writings. One summer I built some furniture pieces with a flat black finish for Else and shortly after that, the Farm asked me to build the simple pole garage that stands next to the tool shed at the Farm—the very first structure that I built. As I recall, there was little or no instruction as to how to proceed and I was left, for the most part, to figure things out on my own. Jane did help me in nailing down the metal roofing and as we worked I shared with her a dream—another first.

A few years after graduating from college, and having worked for nine months as a social worker in Detroit, I returned to Three Rivers. Jane offered to let me live at the hut for the summer in exchange for doing the electrical wiring. At that time it was still a one-room structure without kitchen or bath, so I constructed a simple little "kitchen" on the screened porch. It had a propane camp stove and an elevated 20-gallon plastic garbage can fitted out with a small water spigot at the base for gravity fed "running water." I had to carry the water in buckets from Helen's house!

BUILDING YEARS

It was through Jane Bishop and Paula VanValkenburg that I was introduced to Christopher Alexander and his *Timeless Way of Building*. This *way* focused on a generative approach to making objects that were centered in wholeness. In his attempt to objectify this wholeness and its archetypal patterns in nature and the created world he developed something called *the mirror of the self test*. This test, which is extremely difficult to do, works to link the archetypal reality of our inner *Self* with its "mirrored" objective reality in the material outer world. Alexander used this test as a way to deepen his insights into the creative process and its choices. For me, Christopher Alexander was to building what C. G. Jung was to individuation. These two realities in my life slowly, step by step began to grow me. My work for the Farm and its surrounding community of people was part of the necessary grounding for this growth. Its other aspect was the inner work I was doing with counselors at the Farm.

I am especially aware of the debt of gratitude that I owe to Jane Bishop for her abiding friendship, her love of building and her depth of insight. I think it was through her that I had my deepest experiences of a "timeless way of building." It was life-giving to have this creative work, building and remodeling at the Farm over the years. Everything I did was in some way also building me, whether or not I was conscious of it at the time.

ODE TO TALI

In her autobiography, Helen says,

> I want to pay tribute to a noble dog who was mine
> for only a year or so.... I called him Taliesin after
> the Welsh seer and King's poet...affectionate, yet
> aloof and self-contained, he lived with me for a
> while and then one day...[h]e disappeared. He
> was found two days later in the Priory woods ly-
> ing dead.... The young man (who had found him)
> wrote a touching little poem saying no less than the
> truth—that Tali had meant something indefinable
> to all those who knew him. Later we chose the name
> Taliesin for the guesthouse at Apple Farm.

I think, like this young man, many of us at Apple Farm had an experience of Tali House as something indefinable. For me, Tali was the one building capable of embodying the spirit of the Farm. It was an alchemical vessel of transformation, where its very "dysfunction"— the squeaky floors, thin walls and idiosyncratic plumbing—was, perhaps, part of the very necessity of its alchemy and its work on me. Was Tali not a sort of Asclepian dormitory, an incubator of dreams? Think of all the dreams that got dreamed there, written down and worked on. Tali was initially a schoolhouse, a place of learning and higher consciousness. Tali, too, had a second life in service of the spirit and a new inner knowing. For many who would come to the Farm to stay, entering Tali was a homecoming, a place of warmth, comfort, hospitality, lore—something indefinable.

It is well-documented that I opposed the demolition of Tali House for numerous reasons, but life moves on. With its demolition something of the Farm itself died within me; even as a builder I would not know how to begin to construct a guesthouse to replace what I felt had been lost. In the end, neither people nor buildings can carry the value and meaning of my experience of the Self, that of necessity must be projected outward and then be demolished, in this case in order to be rediscovered within in its eternal and indestructible reality and freedom.

I end with Rumi's poem "The Guest House":

This being human is a guesthouse.
Every morning a new arrival.
A joy, a depression, a meanness,
some momentary awareness comes
as an unexpected visitor.
Welcome and entertain them all!
Even if they're a crowd of sorrows,
who violently sweep your house
empty of its furniture,
still treat each guest honorably.
He may be clearing you out
for some new delight.
The dark thought, the shame, the malice
meet him at the door laughing,
and invite them in.
Be grateful for whoever comes,
because each has been sent
as a guide from beyond.

Helen's A-frame, 1965.

Working at the Farm

GEORGE SEHY

I came to Apple Farm for a weekend in my early years. I was asked by Jane if I wanted to work a little while I was here and I said yes. She told me to go down to Helen's at a certain time, as Helen had need of me. I did go down. Helen needed her window air conditioner removed from the window in preparation for the coming winter. It never occurred to me to look outside to see what supported the unit from falling. Apparently it was the window itself because when I raised the window the air conditioner fell out to the ground, with Helen watching. I went outside and there appeared to be no damage to the unit nor to the bush it had landed on. I wasn't asked to work again.

During another weekend stay, I was in a room at Tali House. I was reading William Horwood's book about moles called *Duncton Wood*. I had brought with me some Sculpey clay and spent a good day and maybe more on making a mole. I finished it and then I needed to bake it in the oven so it would harden. I put the piece into the oven. As I read a book, I began to smell something rather horrible and wondered what it could possibly be. I investigated and found that it was coming from the oven where the clay was baking. I looked in and the mole had turned dark brown which rather pleased me. Unfortunately, I had to leave the piece in the oven a bit longer to finish baking. None of the other guests said anything about the horrible smell. It lasted several hours despite my opening a window to air the room out.

Helen, in the early days, wore her hair in a bun. I never saw her when it wasn't that way. One morning after breakfast in the farmhouse, I went outside to go to Tali House. Two women were standing in the driveway. When the woman who had her back to me turned toward me, I realized it was Helen. Her hair was down. I was horrified. It was as though I had seen her naked. Helen quickly came to me and apologized. She said she had just washed her hair and was letting it dry. I was relieved. I felt afterward how grand she was to apologize.

I recall one time I was a guest at the Farm. All weekend we had heard very loud and disturbing roaring engines as some people had started using Stoldt Road as a drag strip. At brunch, we noticed how silent it was. Jane said that the racers had put down yellow lines at the beginning and end of their quarter mile, but someone had gone and painted another yellow line in the middle between the two lines. We all laughed and said, "Jane, you didn't?" She smiled with a twinkle in her eye, but did not admit to doing it.

Some have asked how I got to be the Farm manager. My reply is, "I couldn't run fast enough!" In her April 10 entry from the "Diary of Vowels" section of *Such Stuff...*, Helen writes, "As long as one is alive one must work...work to attend."

George first came to Apple Farm in 1969.

An early party in the farmhouse.

Gratitude: A Letter

HAL EDWARDS

Don, Elanor and Caroline,

I am re-reading (for the third or fourth time, I suppose) Helen's *Such Stuff as Dreams are Made On,* and have found chapter 10 a veritable soul bath, including deep quiet tears and inner shouts of *thank you!* I honor this epiphany by writing to you here and now.

You two have come to be for me the remaining remnant connections of over three decades of growth, enlightenment and individuation attached to Apple Farm. When I first came to Apple Farm back in the 70s, thanks to my beloved mentor, Morton Kelsey, I experienced the synchronistic timing of my insatiable longing and hunger for the Inner Way and the abundant outpouring of quiet and conscious hospitality exuding throughout the entire community. Slowly, influenced by a deeper knowing, modeled through vital community, my extreme and obsessive extraversion, framed with a compulsively busy lifestyle, I surrendered into more and more wisdom and discernment. A more reflective and contemplative Self emerged. During those years I went through several traumatic and dangerous chapters of family, vocational and personal encounters. I was protected and guided, time and time again, through circumstances and opportunities both unconscious and conscious, into the reflective, healing quietness of a more introverted lifestyle. This changed primal perspectives related to personal meaning, values and commitments. During my reading of chapter six in *Memories, Dreams and Reflections,* just prior to learning about Apple Farm, I had no choice but to surrender to this Inner Voice, giving It permission and priority to navigate me through and beyond the collective forces that dominated the first half of my life.

I still feel the awe and "rightness" that flooded my psyche and body when I first visited the Farm, when I found my way to the little cabin out in the woods, when I sat in the circle of sherry and sharing with Else, Nancy, Jane, Helen, Don, Elanor and precious others who were guests and local community residents. Elanor, the delicate way food was prepared and presented modeled a depth of hospitality and care which remains with me. It was there I first experienced the psychic significance of wisdom and synchronicity awaiting my readiness. I welcomed the rare and nourishing balm nestling and waiting within myth, symbol, literature. I experienced several numinous dreams in the Hut, and in my personal sessions and group sessions over the years I was guided by Helen, Else and Don along my own unique Sacred Way. Not once did anyone mess with my destiny. Not once did anyone at any time neglect to honor and respect my sense of call, my depth of despair, my hard and inevitable lessons, my inspiration, my personal joy, my experience of the Center.

Don, how many times you reached down into your resourceful depths and came up with insights and images and timely nuggets. I can see you now, easing out of your chair, turning to your stash of papers or a bookcase and returning with your appropriate piece of wisdom. Thank you for a lifetime of countless hours of reflection, growth and research that make it possible to connect with those tender threads. I shall never forget what makes such immediate access possible.

And then, during one of my last visits, I met you, Caroline, quite serendipitously just outside your home across the street, at a crucial juncture when I sought for guidance concerning my writing project relating to the spirituality of dreams, which contained Morton's unpublished notes and letters, along with Morton's request that I take that material and publish it as I felt led. Caroline, your wise counsel to "write your own" has proven to be incredibly right on. Since that time I have listened to approximately 2,000 dreams with individuals who find their way to me day after day. Perhaps someday in the future, with years of research and my personal experience listening to dreams, I may be inwardly led through a dream or insight to "write my own." It really doesn't matter anymore. What matters most is that I continue to attend what is mine to do and be, trusting the Inner Voice through my own dreams to guide me along the Way.

Every day when I sit with another person in the sacred soul sanctuary of safety and openness, I experience a secret awareness and a precious sense of awe that have evolved over the years (thanks to Jung, Kelsey, Apple Farm, my own personal contemplative daily practice, the undying soul of the church—all couched in countless synchronicities that continually flow ever so mutually in myriad ways), no matter what teachers and circumstances may come my way. If I might say it in biblical terms, all things do eventually and inevitably work together in Love's Presence (Romans 8:28). The Tao/synchronicity of it all brings each of us into the embrace of Oneness.

This is my imperfect attempt to express my love and gratitude to you, Elanor, Don, Caroline, who remain my Apple Farm remnant.

Grief and Gratitude

Grief and gratitude
will always be
very dependable
friends.

United in
their opposites,
they seamlessly
realize,
connect and
transform
past, present and future
through their
slowly refining
grist
of time,
self-discovery
and
trust in the
Mystery
of Great Mercy.

Our work
is to
embrace
the opposites,
live now,
take the next step,
honor uncertainty,
receive
and
remain awake.

Food, Art, Place, People:
30 Years of Memories

SHERMIE SCHAFER

My first visit to Apple Farm was over 30 years ago. I'd been referred to Helen's books, but had no idea what the Farm would be like. After my first typically wonderful dinner that first eve—including an awesome pie made by Charlotte Smith, the cook for many years—I settled into the Hut in the woods, which became my favorite spot. Rustic, it overlooked a large pond that I could enjoy from the little front porch. Sometimes my dog would accompany me on these "retreats" (though she never shared a dream), and together we took many a long walk. Often we were entertained by the furry critters who danced on (or beneath) the roof.

In time I met many interesting people—at dinners, sherry hours, discussions and lively conversations. I watched the community grow creatively, and was always amazed at how things changed between my visits, even while they maintained the rule of "two hours of quiet after lunch, daily!"—the grounds, the buildings, the people living at the Farm, the apple trees, the chickens, the gardens, the tee-pee and two tiny places built near the woods that offered even more solitude.

For many years Helen herself hosted a sherry hour in her house.

It was always a stimulating time, learning more about her journey, discussing the life of dreams, even current events. I learned bits about England, writers she knew or books she recommended.

My first "dream guide" was Jane Bishop—serious, deep and very much to the point. Once I was lamenting (still at quite a young age) that I was feeling less "productive" than formerly, noticing the beginning of the shifts that come with age and life's experiences. Jane's response: "Trust that anything which is restorative to you *is* productive!" Watching her at play or training her horse or a dog was a lesson in both patience and firmness, and they clearly brought her joy.

I have had much respect for the creativity of those I've met over the years: Don's flowers, his beautiful icons, his writing! All that and more, while living with serious back pain much of the time. Elanor's gorgeous quilts, which appear in various places. And Joan Hector's artistry in glass and watercolor are astounding! I loved Dee's sheep when they used to roam the front pasture; I miss their presence. And Dee's laugh was always infectious! Other creative souls included Nancy Hector, who married later in life, moved to New Mexico, and now, widowed, has a whole new community in which she is again quite active. Kay Heustis, Maureen, Mary Houk and more have added imprints on my psyche. Also Bruce Heustis for his incredible design and building skills around the Farm, and George Sehy who manages several details at a time.

There are also places near the Farm that have enriched me, especially St. Gregory's Abbey. On each visit, I made sure I got to join them for a service, loving the smell of the incense and the quieting of their chants. One Christmas Eve some of the Apple Farm community joined them for Midnight Mass. It was quite beautiful, and followed by a feast prepared by the monks! With a good amount of their wine, the tasty foods and stimulating celebration, I think we were there till 2:00 a.m.

My favorite activity at St. Gregory's was walking their woods: the "Avenue of the Pines," the ponds, meditating on the Pagoda and the large Celtic cross of Jesus in the quadrangle where the graves are. I was heartsick to see the devastation to the property wrought by the tornado in 2011, and also amazed that the quadrangle space appeared untouched.

Another delight for me was the bookstore owned by Joanne Holden, which looked to me like a set from a Fellini film! The outside was covered in homespun signs and posters while inside she sold everything from bait and beer to books, new and used, including Helen's works. I hope her spirit remains in the space. And speaking of books, I made the mistake of finding Lowry's Books in Three Rivers; one could spend a week perusing all the titles and stacks in there. (Now there's a lovely little café inside with healthy food, so one can take a break without stuffing empty calories.)

One favorite memory: an Easter Feast at Apple Farm. I brought a leg of lamb from my father's flock, which Charlotte roasted to perfection. Then we had wonderful sides followed by Charlotte's Lady Baltimore Cake! Helen was dressed stunningly in a gray pantsuit and a charcoal sweater, with a simple silver pendant setting it off. I'd never seen her so lovely.

I also came a couple of summers for canning time: green beans, pears (I think), with aprons I made for the tasks. And always, there were red raspberries in the garden to which everyone helped themselves. I remember people coming (for Helen's birthday?) to clean her house and garden before winter set in, which made me envious of all that help!

I did dream work with Joan Miller for a time, and now I so appreciate her writing the newsletter reporting on all the activities at Apple Farm, and her current series of quotes called "50 Days for 50 Years," which I share with my dream group here.

I've been blessed for several years having Don as my dream guide. I once called him after a momentous waking dream/vision that was to radically change my life, asking him if he thought I was "crazy!" (He did not.) He did say he thought it was time for a radical "break" from my counseling ministry to do a sabbatical, which was particularly challenging financially, but a door opened and I moved to northern Michigan for a year.

At this point Don knows me better than anyone else here, and I am grateful for the richness he offers in his interpretations and reflections with me. I always leave with much to think about as I journey home, and beyond. I'm enriched by his wisdom, his experience and his unique way of being in the world. Sadly, I now remember my dreams much less than earlier in my life.

Apple Farm will always be a touchstone in my psyche. It remains a spiritual focus for meditation, contemplation and inner peace. It has been so for over 30 years and I trust that will be so the remainder of my days and of my dreams! May the community's presence and work continue to be the rich blessing that it has always been.

With love and deepest gratitude,
Shermie Schafer

Sisters Nancy Hector Kurilik and Joan Hector in the Round House.

A Matter of Bread

JOHN HOWIE

When my daughter was very young, she and I would spend afternoons making bread. She mostly patted the dough and ate a bit and spread flour around. We had an abundance of bread, and so I called Apple Farm and talked with Jane. I offered to make bread for the Farm and said that we could give several loaves a week. Jane thanked me for the offer and said that she would get back to me.

Five or six weeks went by and I finally gave up on the notion, simply assuming that it was not the thing to do. Then I received a phone call from Jane and she said that they would be happy to have the bread. Curiosity got the better of me so I asked why it had taken so long to make a decision. Jane said that that they had to consider what it would mean for them not to make the bread.

Sarah and I got busy and started the next batch.

John was first connected to Apple Farm through the men's group in the mid-1980s.

Time Stands Still

GREG LITTLE

My introduction to Apple Farm occurred in the mid-1980s. I was on what I believe was called an introductory weekend with three other Apple Farm neophytes. Many things about my time there have stayed with me and were pivotal in my life, which was on the cusp of middle age at that point. My memories of the people I encountered and particularly Helen Luke are to this day important ones as are the dreams I was given while I was there that first time and on subsequent visits.

Of the many unforgettable aspects of that time, one event stands out. The four of us neophytes were meeting with Helen in the afternoon on the day after our arrival. Just being with her was memorable and I remember her as a presence that far exceeded her physical size. After some time, we were given a 15-minute break. I decided to walk on the grounds and being very conscious of time, I checked my watch to ensure that I would not be late. You need to be aware that I have quite an active complex about being on time, so this was not unusual for me. After a while, I checked my watch and discovered that very little time had passed, so I still had ample time to enjoy the grounds. Shortly after, I noticed one of the other newbies calling me to come back as—horrors of horrors—they were waiting for me. I had kept them all, including Helen, waiting—one of my great fears.

I looked at my watch and realized that it had stopped shortly after I started my little sabbatical. I returned quickly, giving my apologies, and checking my watch again, I noticed that it had started working and continued to keep accurate time the rest of my stay at Apple Farm.

For that brief interlude, time stood still for me—I who have always been very aware of time and being on time. I believe that the one who sends us dreams and synchronicities was giving me that lesson. The trickster was playing with my on-time complex. I still struggle with an overly active desire to be on time, as my wife who has no problem in this regard will attest. However, when this happens, I remind myself of the time when my unconscious conspired for me to keep Helen Luke waiting.

Helen Luke and Catherine Henstis in the Round House.

A New Time

JOAN MILLER

That which first drew me to Apple Farm draws me still. I find here a wondrous meeting of

Well and woe
Old ways and new
Place and people
Feminine and masculine
Psychological and spiritual
Workers and community
Openness and tradition
Scarce money and great riches
Practical and Mysterious

At my first Thursday group ever, the person next to me introduced herself as a member of the Apple Farm Community. "What does being a member of the Apple Farm Community mean?" I asked. She responded, "It means that I do my inner work."

There's a way of listening and seeing in the Farm community that's unlike other communities with which I also affiliate. The devotion which we share is to Apple Farm and to that "ruthless task of individuation" which takes us all to our inner work.

A midwife I know tells me that, while the birth attenders do all in their power to bring the newborn into the world, the newborn has to take its own first breath. I think of the Farm in this latest newly-born time. I wonder if we who love the Farm will be able to both attend and wait for it to take its own first breath. I wonder if we will decide that we will carry it financially. I wonder if we will be able to make the necessary bridges from the memories of its glorious beginnings and founders to the new way that is probably inevitable and will be different. And in the complicated days of transition, I wonder if we will be able to increase the flow of information in ways that serve the whole.

I find I feel excitement about the next thing. From my vantage point of seeing people in farm hours, I find that the Farm continues its invitational work in folks who are new to the Farm. At the same time, I hear vitality in the dreams of persons who have been around for many years—dreams of moving closer and embracing new ways of connectedness to the Farm. How will we know how to move forward in these times?

These words from Helen offer a perspective for this new time at Apple Farm:

> In our moments of choice how do we know that we are obeying the voice of truth? We can only do our best to discriminate our motives, free ourselves from conventional opinions, watch our dreams, use our intelligence, together with our intuition, weigh the values involved and the effects on other people, and then act wholeheartedly from the deepest level we know. If our choice proves to be a mistake, it will be a creative mistake—a mistake leading to consciousness. If it is a question of a big change in our lives, something almost always comes from without to meet the urge from within, and we have a chance to recognize our way—either by resisting a temptation or by accepting a new attitude. If our commitment to our "fate," to the will of God, includes the willing-

ness to pay the full price, we will not go astray—we will relate to the Spirit within, not succumb to possession by it. There is no rule to tell us whether this or that is the right attitude, the right way to behave in all circumstances. (from "The Story of Saul" in *The Inner Story*)

Joan first came to Apple Farm in 1989.

Jane's One-Timers

Mary Powers

The first time I came to Apple Farm was to have tea with Jane and Don. I didn't know who they were, but Joanne Holden told me I had to do it, so I did. I didn't know who she was either, but a Sufi friend had directed me to the Long Lake Food and Book Shop and for many of us, including me, that is where our lives changed.

Tea turned into meetings with Jane and it has all been worth every minute.

One time in a meeting with Jane, she asked how things were going. I made a zigzaggy line with my hand and said, "Which way do I go, which way do I go?" Jane laughed and said, "That is the great mystery, to know which path to take, which decisions to make, which inner voice to listen to. That is why dream work is so important. If we pay attention to our dreams and communicate with them, they will guide us through our days, but we have to be constant."

One time in a visit with Jane, she asked, "What's been coming to you lately?" I said I had been working on a list of items that fell under the categories of either Fire or Water. She was delighted and wanted to know every item and what category it fell under. She really provoked thought about it. That was a great visit.

One time in a meeting with Jane we discussed the word "sin" and how it is really a Spanish word for "without," such as *torta* sin *tomate*, which is Spanish for "sandwich without tomato." The word "sin" took up the whole hour, and we both enjoyed that day.

In one of our visits close to the end, I told Jane that I had been thinking a lot about her and that I would see her, then I would see a running horse. She really laughed hard and said, "Very good, because I have been reading about the life of Sea Biscuit, the racehorse." Then I told her how I was a few minutes late because I had stopped at a garage sale and bought a jewelry box. I hadn't even looked in the box but when I did, I found a sterling silver chain with a pendant of a running horse. That was another very good day with Jane. I gave her the necklace and when she passed, Nancy gave it back to me.

There were so many hours, but not nearly enough. After Jane passed, I started to see little inklings of Jane in other members of the Farm. Now, years later, I see Jane in the constancy necessary to maintain Spirit in a somewhat wild, yet moral manner.

Mary first came to Apple Farm in 1995.

Helen's 90th birthday party in 1994. Pictured, left to right: Kay Henstis, (unknown), Joanne Holden, Maureen O'Malley, Barb Johnson, Elanor Raiche, Glen Williams.

The Inner Light at Apple Farm

MARK NEPO

I first came to Apple Farm in the fall of 1996 to meet Helen Luke, a gift in itself, and quickly met the tribe of inner angels living in community there: Don, Elanor, Jane, Nancy, Janet, Dee and so many others. If our souls are roots growing firmly in the ground of Spirit, those in community at Apple Farm have been quiet farmers of this inner terrain, for half a century. As a result of this remarkable devotion, the Farm has become a palpable place of Spirit. You can feel it wherever you might wander on the land. The love and care of Spirit over decades has made the Earth reveal its presence. If you spend enough time there, you will grow. I know I have.

With gratitude to Apple Farm, I want to share a reflection about how I've grown over the years. I bear witness to all that the Farm has seeded and harvested through the gentle perseverance of wakeful love and care.

THE INVITATION TO GROW

"Why is the road to freedom so long?"
asked a troubled apprentice.

And the master replied,
"Because it has to go through you."

—from an old Zen story

It takes years for seeds to grow into trees and the seasons shape
and scar each tree into place. You could say that the journey of being
a spirit on earth is the human equivalent and the years of experience
shape and scar each of us into place. You could say that this is the
long road to freedom—inner freedom. It is our invitation to grow.

When I was starting out I wanted so badly to become a poet that
I held it in view like some hill I needed to climb to see from. But
getting to the top, something was missing, and so I had to climb the
next hill. Finally, I realized I didn't need to climb to become a poet,
I was a poet.

The same thing happened with love. I wanted so badly to love
and be loved, but climbing through relationships like hills, I realized
again that I was loving and loved all along.

Then I wanted to become wise, but after much travel and study,
it was during my bedridden days with cancer that I realized I was already wise. I just didn't know the language of my wisdom.

Now I understand that all of these incarnations come alive in us
when we dare to live the days before us; when we dare to listen to the
wind singing in our veins. We carry the love and wisdom like seeds
and the days sprout us. And it's the sprouting that's the poetry. It's
the sprouting that's the long road to freedom.

Another lesson comes directly from my time at Apple Farm. It
comes from a conversation I had with Helen. During what turned
out to be our last conversation, she said to me, "Yours is to live it, not
to reveal it." This troubled me, for I have spent my life becoming a
writer, thinking that my job has been just that—to reveal what is essential and hidden.

In the time since Helen died, I've come to understand her last
instruction as an invitation to shed any grand purpose, no matter
how devoted we may be to what we are doing. She wasn't telling me

to stop writing, but to stop striving to be important. She was inviting me to stop *recording* the poetry of life and to *enter* the poetry of life.

This applies to us all. If we devote ourselves to the life at hand, the rest will follow. For life, it seems, reveals itself through those willing to live. Anything else, no matter how beautiful, is just advertising.

This took me many years to learn and accept. Having begun innocently enough there arose separations, and now I know that health resides in restoring direct experience. Thus, having struggled to do what has never been done, I discovered that living is the original art.

Horses

Meister Eckhart says they are the most God-like creatures. No wonder we can be intimidated by them. They're large also. I'm not an expert by any means with or about horses, but I have had a fair amount of experience of and with them over the years.

All creatures, Barry Lopez says, are other nations. We need to read, study and observe them as well as interact with them. What I hope for with a horse is to have a good working relationship with them—a partnership insofar as it is possible. The human needs to have the deciding vote, so to speak. But the horse has a great deal to bring (and sometimes, alas, has the last word). I don't consider the horse, or any animal for that matter, as a pet. They're not here for my gratification. They're here because I love them and want to have as equal a partnership as I can with them. That varies considerably from horse to horse and person to person.

Jane Bishop

Jane and Moon at Apple Farm.

Moon and Sunny

Carol Donnelly

Three Rivers became my home on February 1, 1999. I left Evanston, Illinois on that cold, rainy afternoon and arrived with my yellow lab, Raleigh, in the early evening to rent the barn apartment at Apple Farm while my new home on Day Road was being completed. On June 7, Raleigh and I moved into my unfinished house on Day Road leaving most of my belongings in Bruce Heustis' workshop until mid-July.

Sometime in early spring of 1999, the idea of bringing a horse to Apple Farm in a joint ownership between the Farm and me became a reality. Maureen, Jane and Nancy had been on the lookout for an appropriate animal. I don't remember who found Moon. She had been "rescued" by the owners of a small acreage on Hoffman Road for their young daughter, and although their daughter loved Moon, she was afraid of the white Appaloosa. With some excitement, I went with Maureen and Nancy and Jane to meet the horse. We found her to be gentle, quite beautiful, and at 12 years old, exactly what we were looking for. So we bought her for $700 and she was delivered to her new home, Apple Farm.

How we loved that horse and what good care she received. We worked out a schedule sharing her feeding times, and she was visited by all who came to the Farm. At the time, Rachel, an Appalossa

Quarterhorse who belonged to Lou Noguera, was living at the Farm. Lou frequently came from Holland to groom Rachel and ride her. Although we fed Rachel along with Moon, her disposition was a bit more feisty than Moon's and we were very careful around her. But Rachel loved Lou. Sometimes Lou would ride Moon when he came to the Farm, and sometimes one of us, usually Nancy or I, would ride Moon along with Rachel and Lou. We rode at a leisurely pace along Hoffman Road and through some of the wooded paths behind St. Gregory's Abbey. It was on one of these latter rides that Lou suspected Moon was losing her eyesight. Moon's oncoming blindness was later confirmed by the vet when Moon was around 17 years old.

When Moon had been living at the Farm for about two years, we began to think about breeding her. In the excitement of looking for a stallion, we did overlook the notion of what we would do with another horse. I don't remember who found Sonny, a Quarterhorse Palomino. Sonny was a small but well-built typical Palomino with a yellow coat and a flowing blonde mane and tail. I think Nancy and Maureen went to a farm on Flowerfield Road to have a bridle repaired, and saw him in the pasture there. So they asked me to go look at him, and we agreed that he would sire Moon's foal. In the fall of 2003, we paid the stud fee of $200 and arranged to have Moon delivered there during her next heat. The breeding was successful, and Moon came home, soon showing signs of pregnancy.

On the cold, rainy morning of April 5, 2004, Jean Clampitt, who was staying at the barn apartment, called me very early in the morning to say that she thought Moon was starting to deliver. It was the moment we had been waiting for! With great haste I dressed and raced over to the Farm in time to watch the birth of this tiny, absolutely beautiful foal, deep red with gorgeous white blanket on her withers and her father's blond ruffle of a mane and short tail. This is what every Appaloosa breeder hopes to see! Wet and bedraggled, Moon was the perfect mother. We didn't know the foal's gender until a few days later when the vet arrived and confirmed that we had a colt. Since Nancy had informed me that they had decided the colt belonged to me (a mixed blessing), I was to choose his name.

Among a lot of suggestions, I decided his official name would be "Moon Sun," to be called Sunny.

We were to have our difficulties with Sunny. Before he was weaned, he stepped on a nail that became embedded in his coffin, and he had to be transported to the clinic in Cassopolis along with Moon, for surgery on his foot. Then he was confined to a stable at the Farm for a few weeks for healing, and that did not make this energetic young colt a happy horse. It took several of us, along with Norm, to change his dressing every day. Eventually we had to wean him because the stall was too small to protect Moon from becoming a victim to his coltish behavior. A few months after his leg healed, Sunny once again got into trouble when he ran into a piece of rusted metal fencing and suffered a large gash on his left shoulder. This time with the help of Cindy Heustis, I dressed his wound every day and again he recovered.

Sunny grew into a beautiful young horse and responded well to several month-long training sessions with Dave McCarthy. Eventually, realizing that he had to be ridden and could no longer stay at the Farm, he was leased for a short time, and then sold to a woman who lives just off Dutch Settlement Road in Cassopolis. It was very difficult to part with Sunny, but his time with me had to end.

Sunny's story goes on, as does Moon's, but suffice it to say that this chapter of my life with Apple Farm was a childhood dream come true, that of having a horse and learning the adventures of caring for one. The dream was embellished with the reality of sharing the first seven years of Sunny's life and learning about horse care from Jane, Nancy, Maureen and others. I think that Moon and Sunny gave a great gift to Apple Farm in those years as so many guests had the joy of relating to them on their visits to the Farm. Eventually, following Jane's death, Nancy's move to New Mexico and Maureen's retirement from the Farm, Moon moved to my back yard on Day Road where she happily munches grass and gives pleasure now to the guests at GilChrist Retreat Center who frequently come down to visit her.

The cast of Seed of Adam, *a play by Charles Williams (c. 1996).*

66

CHRISTMAS 2000

Celebrations in general, and this very particular Christmas celebration right here, right now, keep the Gods alive and give honor to the ancestors. Not only are celebrations enjoyable (and hard work), they are a vital part of life. You find this belief in most cultures. And think, also, this is the first Christmas of the new millennium!

Will something happen this year as happened two thousand years ago at this time of year? Some small thing as natural as childbirth, as momentous as God becoming flesh? Or will it be, say, an extraordinary explosion in earth or sky, mind or heart? God revealed to us yet again in a way we couldn't have imagined. Will we recognize a new manifestation of the Holy any sooner than it was understood who the newborn babe was 2,000 years ago? There were signs and portents but the impact of them faded over time. It was decades later that Christ began showing Himself as the son of God.

Think of it! This new millennium, perhaps a new showing forth of the Godhead. We know spirit lives in all things, all people, all creatures, all of the time, yet comes to us anew over and over again.

The guidance we need, in order to recognize these manifestations, new or old, comes in large part from our ancestors—not just our blood relatives but from all those from any time or place that have called to our spirit, have enlightened or delighted us, been companions, given us support; those and the unborn as well we celebrate tonight. By our coming together in honor of these sacred ones, together yet each of us in our own way, we call upon the Spirits, on that Holy Other to be among us, as we remember and honor and celebrate their Beings.

Let us continue to prepare ourselves as we participate in this celebration, this feast, for God's coming yet again in a new way, in this new millennium.

Jane Bishop

Helen at Christmas, 1973.

The Ghetto

VERA SMUCKER SHENK

I've started working one day a week in southern Michigan at a small farm/retreat center. It has two horses; a "flock" of sheep; five friendly, free-ranging chickens; and five large goldfish in two horse troughs made into a fishpond. Working there is a way for me to stay in touch with my love of the outdoors. Usually I do grounds work.

Maureen, who's in charge of giving me my duties for the day at Apple Farm, was apologetic from the beginning about the morning's tasks. She said she was taking me to the part of the barn they called "the ghetto." I came that morning prepared for rain. It was cloudy outside, so I was wearing my blue rain suit. She asked if I had dirty clothes, too—and did I have boots? I had both. She took me to the barn, explaining (again apologetically) that cleaning the ghetto was on her list.

We entered through the Dutch-style doors, and she led me to a closed door, which she then opened. Out wafted the smells of strong ammonia; "the ghetto" was an old chicken coop.

Suddenly I was eight years old and standing in the chicken house of my girlhood farm in Ohio. The smells were so familiar—so "chicken house-ish," so farm-like. I was happy and at home at the same time. Dear Maureen was still apologizing and explaining how to do the task: get the wheelbarrow, over there were the rake and the shovel. I actually giggled at her apologies. Apologizing for this? Apologizing for letting me get dirty, for letting me get in touch with my farm self again? No apologies needed! Here I was, in my late forties, giving myself permission to follow my heart enough to let myself be there, to be doing exactly this—physical labor—and getting dirty and smelly and being in the manure and doing a clean-out-the-barn spring cleaning. I was delighted...I was "tickled."

And yes, I was "home." I was tickled because I could picture myself e-mailing my siblings and telling them of my chicken-house day—shoveling out straw and chicken droppings (the ghetto had a chicken-roost stand, so the droppings were mostly in one place) and feeling connected to my rural roots.

It's good to be content with the mundane, good to get dirty and smelly once in a while in a culture that values spray cans of air freshener and dandelion-free, "perfect" green lawns. And it was good to work at Apple Farm that day.

2002

Choice: Essays

Trauma and Choice

MARLENE SARLE

Recently Don Troyer, M.D. and Jungian analyst, introduced the Apple Farm community to Donald Kalsched's recent book, *Trauma and the Soul.* I found that the insights Don presented posed a challenge to pursue more deeply and intently the personal meaning and reflect intellectually and emotionally on the implications. These are some of my reflections, interpretations and conjectures.

A psychologist once said to me that no one comes through childhood unscathed. That seems a reasonable assertion. One might infer, then, that what Kalsched has to say might relate to anyone who comes through childhood, maybe differing in the matter of degree—the intensity and persistence of the trauma. The specific make-up and sensitivity of the child must contribute to the extent and depth of the trauma. Kalsched's intent, however, is toward those who have experienced debilitating childhood trauma. This is a far-reaching book from which any seeker might find applications and meaning for themselves as well as further understanding of loved ones. Professionals in education and human services will recognize Kalsched's descriptions and deepen their understanding of those they serve.

Kalsched's premise is that as a result of childhood trauma, the true self—the pre-trauma, untraumatized, unscathed soul—goes into hiding to protect itself. A pseudo-self develops and becomes a tormentor, an inner persecutor, who persecutes in the name of protection. Its purpose is to keep the true self safe from the onslaught of life. In the introduction to his previous book, *The Inner World of Trauma*, Kalsched describes the defense system of the persecutor/protector. It is an insightful and worthwhile read.

Damage to the traumatized psyche may be clear and obvious, or it may be subtle and hidden. The sins will sooner or later reveal themselves to the victim and/or others connected to the victim. Classic neurosis, addictions, depression and defense mechanisms continue to protect and preserve the true self from further injury and destruction. Trauma victims will often draw back from life (or attack life viciously—as when the victim becomes the perpetrator), afraid to risk engaging life. Taking even reasonable risks and pursuing opportunities are dangerous. This extreme protection of self is in itself re-traumatizing. The persecutor deprives one of a realistic view of self and life, emphasizing negatives while denying positives. The life force seeps away; the victim suffers crippling loss of soul.

Helen Luke once wrote in her journal, "Something in me could easily curl up in a womb and turn my back on life." When she threw the I Ching, it instructed her to work on and set right what has been spoiled. Helen's context may not have been one of traumatized victim, but her description is apt. How we respond on those occasions when we find ourselves curled up is crucial to the outcome and destiny of our souls. She says that "serenity can come, but only by doing the work."

On another occasion, Helen said, "If we cannot stop persecuting ourselves—beating ourselves for what we conceive to be sins within us—then we must go on in complete acceptance of our powerlessness." Finding and taking hold of power—even if it seems so fragile at first—is the first step in confronting the persecutor. Power goes hand in hand with courage. As one taps into the minute bits of courage and power, they will progressively emerge, grow and give strength and support in the confrontations to come. The power that is needed is simply the power to make a choice. Of course, even though that sounds simple, it is not easy—especially for the tortured soul who has little hope for freedom from the persecutor. But as Anais Nin says,

> And then the day came
> when the risk to remain tight in a bud
> was more painful than the risk to bloom.

This risky choice is posed by the "lifegiver," also known as the infinite, the absolute, the mysterious one, God or the Self. We are given the choice to actualize this lifegiver within our own soul. This is the only possibility for healing and wholeness. Kalsched seems to be saying that to reject the offer from the infinite *is* madness, psychosis and narcissistic pathology. He suggests that "all madness is a refusal of life."[1]

That is a frightening proposition and one senses an urgency in its offer. It feels like a life and death ultimatum. However, it seems to me that it is not necessarily a one-time offer. If refused, the offer may be given again. To continue to refuse is surely dangerous. But to choose the lifegiver does not mean the choice will only need to be made once. Especially for the severely traumatized, a lifetime of returning to the choice for life may be necessary. Mark Nepo's description of the "never-ending task of deciding to whom we entrust our life" fits.[2] Will we entrust our life to the true self and encourager or to the false self and tormentor—today, tomorrow, next week?

Hopefully, as one experiences a renewed life force, "yes" to life becomes an easier choice. The strength to return grows and returning becomes more natural. As the true self more and more takes its rightful place in the psyche, it becomes an able promoter of continued "yes" choices. The false self, the persecutor, begins to lose its grip on the tortured soul. Letting go of the symptoms means giving up the protection of the prosecutor. Vulnerability discourages one from coming out of the protector's domain. Then one must again muster one's courage and power to simply say, "I choose life."

When the pain of trauma and loss of soul become intolerable, a "yes" response to the lifegiver is likely to impel the victim into therapy or an alternative environmental community where the "affectively attuned witness" sits with and walks alongside the traumatized soul. When the trauma victim gets a glimpse of the greater purpose and larger meaning, the victim will seek, "the one who hears the cries."[3] This is the beginning of the road to healing and wholeness. This is the healing place, where expression of the trauma is heard. This is where the divine light enters through the cracked, fragmented psyche. When the compassionate witness listens and attends to the broken spirit the space between them is holy ground.

The cracked, fragmented psyche

Endnotes

1. Kalsched, 200.

2. Nepo, Mark. The Book of Awakening. *SanFrancisco: Conari Press, 2000: 67.*

3. Kalsched, 41.

Choice in J.R.R. Tolkien's
The Lord of the Rings

HELEN M. LUKE

Choice is the conscious exercise of free will, and the nature of a man's choices is the measure of his growth to maturity. The great majority of choices made by human beings are really not properly so called at all, but are mere acquiescence in a compulsive desire from the unconscious. "I don't choose to do this or that," is very often a synonym for, "I don't want to do this or that," or, "I am afraid to do it," or, "I can't be bothered." Such a phrase is usually heard in the negative form, and unconsciously the speaker announces a profound truth. Indeed, as he says, he does not choose. If he really had made the conscious decision he means to convey, he might then say, "I choose not to do so and so," instead of, "I don't choose." This kind of choice may often look very decisive and mature but is in fact on the same level as the choices of a child who obeys or disobeys his elders either because he is afraid, or rebellious, or because he is compelled by outer forces or by his instinctive urges.

At the other end of the scale is the free choice of the mature man, made with the highest degree of consciousness possible to that particular individual and with complete acceptance of responsibility

for its consequences whatever they may be. This taking of responsibility must of course include the recognition that, insofar as we
are still possessed by unconscious contents, our choice is not wholly
free and will therefore have unseen consequences which we cannot reject. Nevertheless, if we have made the truest effort of which
we are capable to discriminate the motives, the choice, no matter
how "mistaken," will lead to a situation in which we may be shaken
into greater awareness. As Jung says, although it would be nonsense
to attribute to the unconscious a "purpose" in our conscious sense,
yet the evidence is overwhelming that, provided we will confront it
consciously, with the courage to listen, it will constantly offer us that
which we need for the next step towards individuation and wholeness. The one fatal thing is to sit on the fence, playing for safety by
making no choice at all when we are in doubt.

This brings us to the crucial matter of what we may call a man's
basic choice. A young man said recently, "What does it mean to be
chosen? I don't believe anyone is chosen." He was talking of the
Jews as the "chosen people." The answer surely is that a man (or
a people at a certain moment in its history) is chosen because he
has chosen, because he has made his fundamental choice between
drifting with the many or relating *as an individual* to the collective
forces of consciousness or of the unconscious, of opinion or instinct.
The Jews were a chosen people because, in a hostile world, they had
glimpsed the one God and held to their vision through all persecu-
tion and backsliding. A man is chosen, is one of "the elect" because
he chooses to follow the One by the way of individual consciousness.
Immediately, however, a great temptation arises. To be chosen in
this sense is confused with being set above one's fellows, with being
"special," not in the true sense of the word, which means simply "of
a particular kind, distinct from the generality," but in the sense of
being specially good or meritorious. The extreme dangers of this
are seen in the excesses of the Calvinistic doctrine of the elect, the
saved. Once a man was pronounced "saved"—perhaps after a most
genuine inner experience, he was beyond the law and could slip into
justifying himself no matter how unconscious his following choices.

"Love and do what you will!" But when a man feels in himself, after a glimpse of the real nature of Love, that he has made his fundamental choice, he must immediately remind himself that his choice is not a sudden release from responsibility but, on the contrary, imposes on him the necessity for a life-long effort to renew daily this choice in every smallest detail. He may more safely say to himself, "I have chosen to learn what love is, and therefore for a very long time I must *give up* doing what I will—that is, making unconscious compulsive choices—on the superficial level, in order to follow this deepest will in me to love, to be true to my individual way for which I am chosen, set apart." Only when individuation is achieved will come the state in which the innocence of the child and the conscious will become one thing. Most of those who have made this basic choice can remember a major turning point in their lives when it became a fully conscious act of will, though we may not have realized the crucial nature of the decision until afterwards. For it may concern a choice about something which from outside does not appear to be a vital matter at all.

> To some among us comes that implacable day
> Demanding that we stand our ground and utter
> By choice of will the great Yea or Nay.

—C.F. Cavafy

"By choice of will"—not by choice of desire or fear.

The Lord of the Rings provides us with a great wealth of examples of these things—images which can stay with us and change us, when the effort of all this thinking about the nature of choice slips away, as the effect of words alone must always do.

The theme of human choice runs through the book like a thread, as indeed it must in any account of the meaning of human life. All the nine companions are of course "chosen ones"—men of good will in the literal sense of the words, who have said "yea" to the crucial choice and who are therefore forced to the constant effort to make conscious rather than unconscious choices. Those who say "nay" are represented by the nine riders and Gollum and Saruman. The nine Ringwraiths were human beings, and they had, on the "implacable day" made free choice, but having said a conscious "no," they have gradually become nothing but wraiths with no power of choice left anymore, totally subservient to the commands of the dark power in the unconscious which forbids all individual growth.

In Gollum, humanity remains. Choice is still open to him because he has been *swallowed* by the power of the Ring, he has not deliberately given up his will to the use of power over others. His devotion to the "Precious," terrible and dangerous as it is, is still devotion to something outside himself for which he will give up everything else. It is a hot thing, not a cold intellectual drive to power as in the Ringwraiths, and can inspire a deep pity. As long as any trace of humanity remains, the possibility of the basic choice recurs again and again, but with each evasion it becomes more difficult. Gollum is offered the great chance, through Frodo's compassion, to give his devotion to a man, a person, the only thing which can possibly save any one of us from the power of the "Precious," the Ring of power, which will gradually become more deadly within us each time we refuse to commit ourselves to a relationship. One of the most tragic images in the book is surely the moment when Gollum, still not quite committed to his intended treachery, looking for an instant like an old and weary hobbit, touches the sleeping Frodo with tenderness. The choice hangs on a hair—and then Sam wakes and out of *his* devotion to Frodo and fear for him, he orders Gollum off with rough words—and Gollum's last chance of conscious choice is shattered. Who can blame Sam in his simplicity? He repents and he pays in full, and perhaps it is through this mistake that he began to understand Frodo's compassion, and so, when it comes to that last crucial choice of his on Mount Doom, he does not kill Gollum, and thus the world was saved.

In Saruman, the case is different again. He is a man of a high degree of insight and wisdom who having said, it seemed to himself and others, the basic "yea" and grown to great stature—a chosen one, a guide—subsequently betrays this choice. His guilt is therefore infinitely greater than Gollum's. The latter's single-minded devotion to the Ring becomes in the end a means to the final deliverance, and one has the strongest feeling that, falling into the fire, his old life will burn away and that he will emerge to a new life beyond it. But with Saruman no such possibility exists. He has betrayed the light of consciousness and used it for personal power, and when he is offered chance after chance of choosing again he prefers to cling to the meanest and most petty forms of power rather than humble his pride. Nevertheless he is still human and choice remains. At the very last the opportunity comes again. First Gandalf, then Frodo offers it to him. His refusal brings death at the hands of his own slave, and he is seen to dissolve into smoke, nothingness, as did the Ringwraiths—a very different symbol from Gollum's death in the purging fire.

Now let us follow a few of the innumerable choices which face along the way those who have "stood their ground" and uttered "the great Yea." One could say that all the choices made by the hobbits up to the moment of the irrevocable "yes" at Rivendell and the beginning of the conscious quest are the half-conscious ones which nevertheless spring from the potential "yes" in a person, his fundamental goodwill and capacity for accepting responsibility for his true feeling. The early choices of Sam, Merry and Pippin are made out of their feeling for Frodo, their loyalty and friendship, and out of the light-hearted love of adventure in generous young hearts. They have no notion of where this first choice will lead them, as mercifully we have not either at the beginning, or we would never have the courage to start. But they are true to what they know at the moment—their love for Frodo and the responsibility it involves. They will not let him go alone into danger. And from this choice they are led, stage by stage, into awareness of the tremendous issues involved and to the acceptance of all the necessities of the way. For Sam, to be near his master is his greatest happiness and he does not therefore make any really conscious choice until he stands before the gates of Moria and must decide alone whether to part with his

beloved pony or his beloved master. It is his first conscious separa-
tion from purely instinctive action. He chooses consciousness and
so is led step by step to his moments of fully responsible choice at
Minas Morgul. For hearts such as these, wrong choices, though they
remain wrong, are nevertheless an essential part of the pattern, and,
once *accepted as wrong,* they may be seen as a vital necessity. Pippin's
choice to indulge his curiosity over the Palantir brings near disaster
but in fact serves to mislead the enemy and gain vital time. Because
of his basic choice he accepts his guilt, though at first he makes that
well-worn excuse, "I didn't know what I was doing!" "Oh yes you
did," answers Gandalf. Had he not admitted this, if he had clung
to self-justification or to morbid remorse, he would inevitably have
gone on to greater betrayals. Sam's choice to carry the Ring himself
when he thinks Frodo dead is a reversal of his whole nature, an act
of enormous courage, which, though wrong, for it is not his job, is an
absolute necessity whereby the Ring is saved. But it would certainly
not have been saved if Sam had not, within a very few minutes, rec-
ognized that his decision had been all wrong for him, and if he had
not gone back to his master's side. So must we all be ready in extrem-
ity to make choices against the whole trend of our nature, if we are
ever to be absolutely true to the quest, and also ready to recognize at
once when we find ourselves out of our depth, or on the wrong road,
or untrue to our individual way. If Sam had not made that "mistake,"
not only would the Ring have been found on Frodo, but Sam could
not possibly have rescued him, for he owed that chance to the invis-
ibility the Ring gave him. The vital thing is to choose—to choose
with all our heart—and if the heart be pure, it is no matter whether
the choice is "right" or "wrong."

Boromir is an example of a noble and brave heart which nevertheless harbors a secret reservation. He accepts, but he is not wholly
committed. He is someone acting out of devotion, but his devotion
is not to a person, it is to his country, his city. He is capable, as are
millions of people, of making the uttermost sacrifices for the cause
he loves, for the fight against evil, in order to serve that cause. So we
may see how much more surely the motives of the heart are purged

by love of, commitment to, a person, than by love of a cause, however unselfish. For since devotion is given to something collective rather than to something individual, man is blinded to the vital truth that to use collective tools even to the highest end will eventually produce the very evil which he has so nobly fought. For only the individual can transcend the opposites. The collective good and evil are one in the end. Galadriel, the purest of the pure, when Frodo offers her the Ring, replies:

> "The evil that was devised long ago works on in many ways, whether Sauron himself stands or falls. Would not that have been a noble deed to set to the credit of his Ring, if I had taken it by force or fear from my guest?
>
> "And! now at last it comes. You will give me the Ring freely! In place of the Dark Lord you will set up a Queen. And I shall not be dark, but beautiful and terrible as the Morning and the Night! Fair as the Sea and the Sun and the Snow upon the Mountain and dreadful as the Storm and the Lightening! Stronger then the foundations of the earth. All shall love me and despair!...
>
> "I pass the test," she said, "I will diminish and go into the West, and remain Galadriel."
>
> ...Then Sam said, "If you'll pardon my speaking out, I think my master was right. I wish you'd take this Ring. You'd put things to rights. You'd make some folk pay for their dirty work."
>
> "I would," she said. "That is how it would begin. But it would not stop with that, alas! We will not speak more of it. Let us go!"

The greater and more wise the individual becomes, the more dangerous is the great temptation to use power over people for their good. Christ's temptation in the wilderness was just this, and comes always at the moments of greatest threat from the Dark Lord. Gandalf refuses, Galadriel refuses, Aragorn and Faromir refuse, but Saruman, Denethor and, briefly, Boromir succumb.

In Lothlorien the Lady Galadriel looks long and deeply at each member of the Company in turn, and when they discuss it afterwards each says that in those moments there was set before him his fundamental choice, as though the Quest and all it involved were set against his most powerful longings, and each one was forced to confirm his choice. All passed this test except Boromir who speaks of the experience thus:

> Maybe it was only a test and she thought to read our thoughts for her own good purpose; but almost I should have said that she was tempting us, and offering what she pretended to have the power to give. It need not be said that I refused to listen. The Men of Minas Tirith are true to their word.

Galadriel herself calls this the testing of the heart and it is interesting to know that one of the derivations of the word "choice" is a Gothic word meaning "test." It is most significant that Boromir does not say, "I am true to my word," but, "The men of Minas Tirith are true to their word." He has not yet made his final choice, and so at the Falls of Rauros he is possessed by this collective so-called good and he breaks the promise and tries to seize the Ring from Frodo by force. But the corruption has not yet taken irrevocable hold. Awakening from the possession, he is horrified by what he has done and sees in a flash his delusion, then goes at once to the redeeming act: he gives his life for the *individual* value to save the lives of Merry and Pippin, his friends, and so does far more to defeat the Dark Lord than if, refusing his guilt, he had thought, as well he might, "Minas Tirith needs me. These little halflings are of no value in the great fight." As it was, when dying, he confesses to Aragorn what he has done and says, "I have failed." But Aragorn can say to him, "You have conquered. Few have gained such a victory. Be at peace! Minas Tirith shall not fall." Boromir has made his total choice. Late or soon, it is the same. Denethor, his father, greater in power and insight, more fatally possessed, has a like moment of final choice at his end, but fails and dies by his own hand.

The choice of Beregond of the Guard in Minas Tirith is of a kind which touches all of us very nearly. Every man at some point or other of his life must surely be confronted with such a choice. It is the conflict of loyalties. Beregond has freely taken an oath of obedience which is binding in all circumstances, and he is faced with a choice between that oath, which is the absolutely valid basis of his chosen way of life, and loyalty to a person whom he loves, the symbol of the individual values of the heart. He chooses the latter in full conscious-ness of the fact that his choice will mean for him death, probably, or at best disgrace, and the ruin of his career.

The values at stake are not always so clear-cut for us. Every con-scious and responsible man will obey the laws of his community. He recognizes that, by accepting the security and order which it gives him, he binds himself to serve it and to respect its basic rules, unless he should be faced with a choice between this service on the one hand, and loyalty to a deeper, a truly individual value, on the other hand. Thousands of young men today are confronted with a choice about the Vietnam War which they feel to be of this nature. It is easy for them to say, "The war is bad, therefore I will not take part," which is a purely collective statement and in no way absolves them from their observance of law. The crucial question for each man is, "Am I making this decision with full conscious responsibility and with will-ingness to suffer the consequences both outwardly and *inwardly*?" It is very easy indeed to put ourselves above the law on all sorts of issues, either imagining for ourselves lofty motives to cover a weak evasion, or deriding the law as foolish and unjust, to be set aside whenever possible when there is no danger of discovery. Examples of the latter are breaking speed limits or evading taxes. Steinbeck in his *Winter of Our Discontent* shows the deadly nature of the socially acceptable small corruptions. It is equally easy to hide behind loyalty to law and order as an excuse for blindness to the horrors of what is being done in its name, as happened on a huge scale in Nazi Germany. As with Beregond, the choice to disobey must be made only when we see without question that the spirit of the law itself has been betrayed by those who impose it, as it was by Denethor. Even then the law remains the law, and the true justice meted out by Aragorn does not condone the breaking of it, while rewarding the man who dared to choose love.

O n Gandalf and Aragorn, the great ones, the leaders, lies the terrible responsibility, fully realized, of almost daily choices affecting the lives not only of their friends but of the whole outcome of the struggle. Sometimes a choice is forced on them by necessity as at the passage of Moria, and as so often in all our lives, it is still a choice. To *choose* necessity is a very different thing from acquiescing with resentment or with hopeless resignation to the inevitable. We can learn from their choices that no amount of wisdom or good will or devotion can guarantee us against mistakes. Gandalf makes a most costly mistake in choosing to go to Saruman when summoned, instead of going straight to the Shire to urge Frodo to start his journey, and Frodo is consequently *almost* too late—almost, not quite; that seems to be the inevitable theme of man's struggle. Myth, legend, real storytelling, many of the deeper dreams of all of us, show the battle almost lost, or the choice made at the last possible moment. Only later do we see that the mistake made in good faith is a vital part of the journey. Had Gandalf not made this mistake he would not have known of Saruman's treachery, and this could well have been fatal.

From Gandalf's and Aragorn's choices, much can be learned of the way in which a fully responsible choice must be made. Never can it be valid if it comes from the head alone, any more than from instinct alone. A conscious choice must spring from the clearest possible discrimination of the issues involved. We must listen to the arguments of reason and common sense. We must recognize, bring to consciousness, our desires and fears, and only then will we be able to hear the verdict of the heart. For if there is anything that stands out more clearly than all else in the vital choices of this book, it is that the right choice springs always from the heart—the word being used here to mean, not the seat of emotions, but the place where cold intellect and the hot desires meet, are honored, and then unite in true objective feeling. To this discrimination, this listening, must be added the refusal to influence the choices of others, together with courage to take responsibility for choices involving others when it is clear that one has been chosen to lead or guide. Here are some examples of these things. Aragorn at the Falls of Rauros is faced with perhaps his most difficult choice of all. Shall the Company go south to Minas Tirith or east towards Mordor direct or shall he divide the fellowship? His first decision is that Frodo must be free to make his own choice alone. Then when Frodo has left them to seek his answer, Aragorn discusses with the others the various possibilities. All of them except Sam and Aragorn vote for Minas Tirith, for common sense and desire, yet all of them except Boromir are true to the heart values and will follow Frodo if he chooses to go east, though they are determined to stop him, to influence him, if they possibly can. Thus they show their immaturity. In this pass, it is Sam who sees most clearly in his simplicity. Because of his single heart and mind in his love for Frodo, he knows his master's dilemma, knows that there are no two ways for Frodo, but he is terrified and is seeking courage to go where he must go and to go alone. Sam's innocent wholeness and Aragorn's conscious wisdom meet, and now, as so often in our lives in these moments of confusion and hesitation when we strive to find the right choice, Fate intervenes—something comes from outside which makes the direction clear. Boromir's action decides Frodo and he leaves, alone with Sam, for the East; the Orcs attack and capture Merry and Pippin; Boromir is killed, and Aragorn, Gimli and Legolas are left to make the choice alone—to follow Frodo or to go after the Orcs to the help of Merry and Pippin. "Maybe," says Gimli, "there is no right choice." "Let me think," says Aragorn. "And now may I make a right choice and change the evil fate of this unhappy day." After a silence, the light breaks and Aragorn says,

> I would have guided Frodo to Mordor and gone
> with him to the end, but if I seek him now in the
> wilderness, I must abandon the captives to torment
> and death. My heart speaks clearly at last: the fate
> of the Bearer is in my hands no longer. The Com-
> pany has played its part. Yet we that remain cannot
> forsake our companions while we still have strength
> left. Come! We will go now...we will pass on by day
> and dark.

What a powerful image all this is of the wisdom of the heart in a great man! Aragorn abandons almost at once the counsel of his head and his desire, both of which would have chosen to go to his beloved city, to his kingdom, to fight with the "sword that was broken," to fulfill the prophecies. They weigh not at all in opposition to his loyalty to Frodo's freely taken decision. But vastly more important though Frodo's safety is than the lives of two small insignificant hobbits by all rational standards, yet his heart speaks clearly. To abandon friends to torment and death for the sake of a greater "good" would be to subscribe to the values of the enemy, to bring his power even into the heart of the King, and so to make the victory of the dark next to certain. On such issues does the battle hang. Aragorn's decision seems bound to take him out of his way. To delay his essential coming to Gondor could be called a betrayal of his great task. The reverse is true. His choice leads him straight to the meetings with Eomer, with Gandalf, and on to his greatest test, his choice to follow the Paths of the Dead, where all the powers of the unconscious are roused to do battle at his command and so save the day at Minas Tirith.

Gandalf's part in the redemption of Theoden illumines brilliantly the responsibility of a conscious man to one less conscious when this other is faced with a moment of choice. Theoden's will has been undermined and he is wholly dominated by the soft words and lies of Wormtongue. There seems no hope that the king would choose to send the might of Rohan to the help of Gondor. At this point Gandalf takes full responsibility for interfering, for using his own conscious power to break the spell of Wormtongue, so that Theoden comes to himself once more. But this is not enough, is never enough. Theoden, when separated from Gandalf, would only have fallen back again into his weakness, and worse, maybe. His true redemption can only come by his own free and unaided choice. So Gandalf deliberately leads him to Saruman, to Wormtongue's master, whose honeyed words can woo the strongest and there Gandalf stays completely silent, offers no help at all in spite of the enormous issues at stake. Theoden must meet his shadow, make his choice alone and free. We may—indeed we often must—take responsibility for breaking the spell of the unconscious for another, but never may we force him to a choice.

Finally, in the choices of Frodo, the Ring Bearer, the one chosen to carry the greatest of all burdens, we may trace his growth from the simplicity of unconscious goodwill, through darkness and suffering, to that state in which the light shines through him unhindered for those with eyes to see as Sam saw it when they came to the gates of Mordor. Frodo's early choices are simply the acceptance of dark necessity, inevitable choices because of that simple human truth and kindness which are already the mainspring of his nature. Gandalf convinces him that no one else can take charge of that which fate has given to him, without great danger to many people, and so he starts his journey.

> "I wish I had never seen the Ring!" cried Frodo. "Why did it come to me? Why was I chosen?" "Such questions cannot be answered," said Gandalf. "You may be sure that it was not for any merit that others do not possess; not for power or wisdom, at any rate. But you have been chosen, and you must therefore use such strength and heart and wits as you have."

He is already willing, we may note, to go alone, would ask no one else to share the danger. In this perhaps is a clue to the fate which had chosen him. He is that rare thing, a man willing to walk alone. At Bree he makes a semi-conscious choice, which shows how far he is as yet from realizing, except in his head, the danger and profound seriousness of his journey. He chooses to join the party in the Inn parlor, for he has not yet learned that on this quest there can he no "joining the party," no letting up for him—that is, no forgetting, for a brief moment of comfortable merging with the collective. Frodo, whose intentions are excellent when he offers to sing for the company (to prevent Pippin from talking indiscreetly), is caught by the enthusiasm of his audience, begins to show off and literally falls off the table *into* the Ring; his finger just slips into it and he becomes invisible. So do we lose our identity whenever we are thus caught in collective attitudes or emotions through our love of prestige or of being a "good mixer." By this choice Frodo *almost* wrecks the whole quest at the outset. But again the "almost" is "not quite," and instead, his fall into the unconscious is the means of his awakening to a far greater awareness.

At Rivendell, after having been wounded by the Ringwraith, pierced by knowledge of the dark, after the dark power has *almost* killed him, Frodo comes to the "implacable day" of his crucial choice. After such a wounding the days of instinctive choosing are over. For every choice after this we must bear conscious responsibility. The Council has explored all possibilities. It has become clear that there is only one hope of final success—to take the Ring to the fire that forged it—and silence falls on all the wise. Into the silence comes Frodo's voice, "I will take the Ring." His voice seems to issue from him without his volition. In fact so deeply has he consented with his will that no act of will is necessary—that which is both immanent and transcendent has taken over. From that moment on he never again is faced with a choice of direction. Even at Rauros, as Sam saw, that was not in question. His daily-to-be-repeated choice is to lie in the battle against the temptation to put on the Ring, to identify with it, as it grows more and more powerful the nearer it approaches to Mordor and this makes a greater demand on his strength than all the hardships of the way. One may guess that in Galadriel's test it was this choice that came to Frodo's mind.

There is however another moment of absolutely vital choice. It looks of much less significance than the choice at Rivendell, but it comes much later on the way, which indicates its great depth of meaning in human life, and it is not by chance that it is of exactly the same kind as Aragorn's choice after the capture of Merry and Pippin. It is the choice between human compassion on the one hand and all the indispensable arguments of common sense, of justice, of the importance of the quest before everything else on the other. He will not kill the contemptible, dangerous Gollum, and as with Aragorn, the choice is that which saves all. How far Frodo has grown from the hobbit who left the Shire can be clearly seen if we look back to his conversation about Gollum with Gandalf at the beginning. "Why wasn't so disgusting a creature killed?" asks Frodo. "Why did you let him live to escape and be a constant danger? He deserved to die." Gandalf rebukes him. He tells him that Bilbo's mercy to Gollum had ensured his taking little hurt from the ownership of the Ring. There is still a small chance for Gollum to change—that he is very old and very wretched. "Do not be too eager to deal out death in judgment, for even the very wise cannot see all ends." It is a very long and painful road from simple impulses of easy pity or righteous resentment to the depths of positive human compassion which is a very mature thing indeed. At the final dangerous moment when Sam has Gollum at his mercy and lifts his sword in rage to punish his treachery, the issue is the same in essence, though this time the choice is not between head and heart but between instinctive emotion and heart. Sam, too, has won through to compassion. For the simple servant and the plain soldier, for the great king and the hobbit Ring-bearer, for the seers and the wise, the test is one.

And now at the very last, the crowning moment of the myth, at the edge of fulfillment, Frodo succumbs to the Ring. And he uses the very words with which we began this discussion: "I do not choose now to do what I came to do." Indeed he relinquishes in that moment his power of choice. "I do not choose any longer. I abandon my will to the unconscious." Frodo could have become a Ringwraith. The reader is shocked from his high point of joy and pride in the indomitable courage and strength of a great human being into recognition of the fallibility in the last resort of the human will. But it is now, in this final weakness that Frodo is "delivered from evil"—not by his own strength of mind and purpose but by means of him whom he himself has delivered in the deep compassion of his heart. We may think here of Charles Williams' doctrine of exchange and the mystery of the coinherence. In *The Lord of the Rings*, the mystery lives.

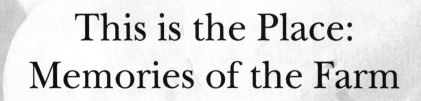

This is the Place:
Memories of the Farm

The Tali Experience

In 2011, we said goodbye to Tali House after severe storm damage. We honor this significant space now with a few of the memories that made their home there, knowing that there are many others as well.

Florence Riley

First I remember Helen's beautiful dog named Tali.

In 1963 or '64, I had come down from North Bay to have "hours" with Helen. My appointed time for that day coincided with the time the old schoolhouse was to be transported down Hoffman Road to become Tali House in honor of Helen's dog who had been shot and killed and was found in a field of the Abbey farm.

So Helen and I drove out to the site and watched the loading, then followed the transport down Hoffman Road to its designated location—supposedly having an "hour" as we drove.

Many years later when I was living in the woods in the house that Dee and Mark now live in, I was seeing people for dream work in the east room, which was an addition on Tali House (the room Kay Heustis lived in for her last years). One afternoon I came home late, had dinner and went to bed. Around 2:00 a.m. I woke up and thought, "Where is Greta?" Then I realized I must have left the dog in the east room. So I walked in the dark through the barnyard and over to Tali House. There she was, lying patiently on the floor and mighty glad to see me.

MAUREEN O'MALLEY

On my first visit to Apple Farm, coming to stay for four nights, and knowing *only* that there were wise women living there, I had tea with Helen Luke before her fire. What I remember is that she spoke of dreams, and I told her I had never had one. I was 32 years old. She suggested that I have a pen and paper near my bed in the event of my having a dream, and told me we would meet again.

That night, in my small room on the first floor of Tali House, I prepared for sleep, paper and pen beside me, and turned out the light. Near 1:30 a.m., I was wakened by what must be—a dream? And I should turn on the light and write it down? And so I did, feeling uneasy with this new occurrence. I was soon back asleep.

In another couple of hours I had a second dream. Of course I wrote it down, feeling very creepy at this middle-of-the-night activity. Immediately I turned out the light, comforted by the lovely red comforter on my bed.

Barely back to sleep, I was startled awake by a noise outside my room. Was this another dream? I was not sure, and, very frightened, I clearly remember pulling the comforter over my head. Not only frightened, but also very tired, I could not possibly try to figure out this *sound*. The comforter again cared for me.

I did sleep again, and I did have another identifiable dream. No dreams for 32 years; now three in one long night.

The next morning at breakfast in the farmhouse, sleepy and feeling unsettled, I learned that another guest, Walter, was staying above me in Tali House. He told a bit of *his* night. In the middle of the night, his dog, who was staying with him, had fallen through a trap door on his room's floor. He had landed in the hall below. Frightened, he had raced back and forth for ten minutes or so until Walter could come down to help him. So this was the noise I heard. What a

relief for me to hear this very natural explanation: not a dream, but a dog.

I did meet with Helen again before her fire and we looked at the three dreams. This "way" was new to me, and when I left Tali House and Apple Farm on Sunday I was not at ease.

I did know that the people seemed very real,
that they were kind to me and I liked them,
and that I had made a date to visit again.

KAYE KOCH

How does one begin to describe the Tali House experience? I remember loving care for details, luxurious comfort without luxury, welcoming and soothing no matter how unsettled and weary the seeker. My first visit to Tali House was in autumn of 1987. I was assigned to the apartment. As soon as I walked in the door, I realized this was exactly where I needed to be. I had found the place I did not know I was looking for. I recall Bruce Heustis remarking that each space in Tali House had its own gift to give. I had not experienced all of the rooms at that time, but I know now he was right on. Tali House accomplished exactly what Tali House was meant to do: house us, comfort us, shelter us as we heal. As it is with us mortals, Tali House bows to old age and infirmity and steps aside to make space for something new. But we will never forget or replace Tali House.

KAREN BRANNAN

December 16, 1998—I am at the Apple Farm. The name is perfect. I remember how I used to draw all those apples all the time—my symbol for inner wholeness, my search for inner and outer wholeness. I am eating an apple. This tiny apartment is so perfect—all that one person ever really needs. Some have little huts in the woods here, like the one in my dream with Sallie, the poet. I wonder...?

The horse is named Rachel. The guesthouse where I am is called Tali for Taliesen. There was a dog named Tali who died. Last night on the Capitol Limited overnight train from D.C., I dreamed of a dog. I was met at the stop in Elkhart, a lovely old refurbished station, by a woman named Joan, whose maiden name was Yoder, who said that my dear friend Ann Raber and her mother Elizabeth Yoder had been very good friends. Already I feel connected.

Three geese flew overhead as we pulled in the driveway. The Apartment, as it is called, is mostly browns, beiges and terra cotta veering toward orange. There's a tiny, perfect little kitchen in red, white and blue and a tiny tub that I manage to fit quite neatly into with just the right amount of hot water. A great window with a Big Mama chair and two bird books and binoculars on the table next, several bird feeders out the window and a patch of woods. Blue jays, cardinals, finches, chickadees, a Siamese cat, some wonderful, huge chickens that range freely in the woods and something in the distance that is either an eagle or a hawk—I feel like Goldilocks who has finally found the place that is "just right." In the Round House, they have a huge collection of paperback mysteries. I suppose they'll enjoy a real-life mystery as well, perhaps help me to solve it.

In the afternoon, 1:30-3:30 is quiet time (it's all quiet time, I learn). I sat and sat and sat in front of the window, listened to Brahms and Mussorsky, slept a bit, poached two fresh eggs, bright orange yolks and had them on toast. The fridge contained exactly the kind of bread I like, baby carrots, sweet gherkins, good coffee. On a shelf, I spied Vienna sausage and ate some for lunch along with cheese, pickles, carrots, apple. All my favorite childhood foods are here: a small tin of peaches, peanut butter (beware!). I am so totally comfortable they might have to drag me out of here. Of course I am thinking of all the people I want to call and say, "Come on up," then wonder if my sister would be able to sit still here. I feel almost stunned with peacefulness. Reading Helen. Meditating. Examining the difference between the outside through the lighter frame of the glass and that through the darker frame. The rooster crows at various times throughout the day. All these things take me back: to Hamilton, to Cataula, to Big Mamma, to G'mamma—to a simpler, quieter time when it was possible to sit and stare and wonder and be glad.

Note: This reflection was written almost 13 years ago. Since then I have visited the Farm several dozen times, often for as long as two or three weeks. Someday I hope to write in full the magnificent journeys I have taken there, in the dark of night, and the light of day, through dreams, contemplation, groups and counseling. I carry the Farm within me now, eat of her apples daily, and still eagerly await my every visit.

JIM CAROW

Tali House has been my retreat home in the last few years. Over the course of five retreats, it has been a home and the place of many hours of reflection and prayer. It has been an inviting and comforting place. It has seen me through a period of deep distress and inner turmoil. On retreat in 2009, I experienced a fearful awakening that prompted a redirection of my inner life. Since then I have been emerging from that period of deep distress and reconnecting with life and spirit.

Tali House has been a vehicle in this healing process. It conveys an aura of warmth and home. It invites and heals. The many icons speak softly and clearly of the healing and inspiring spirit that is present there. I am very grateful to Tali House itself and the many people and their efforts that have sustained it. It has been a great gift.

SCRAPS

Does it seem rather futile and like busy work to pick up a few scrap pieces of lumber and put other odds and ends into the scrap trailer? Let me tell you it is not. To pick up the scraps, however few, is a real contribution toward breaking, what seems to me to be, the American apathy toward waste. You have done more in the battle than save a few bits of lumber. You have made a statement that whatever our society at large may feel about the expendability of resources. You know that they are limited and you value them. Multiply your act by a million and a significant savings, as well as a significant statement has been made. It may never be heard in the lobbies of Congress, no notice in the local paper may be made, but you will know you have done what you as one individual can do. You have acted on a belief. You have done more than criticize or moan or bewail the sad state of affairs in our country or in the world. You have acted. You have broken the chain of indifference and apathy.

Jane Bishop

Helen, Elanor, Don and Else on Don and Elanor's wedding day (1968).

Remembrances

ELANOR RAICHE

Why ruin a good question with an answer?

—The Talmud

ANIMALS

Names have been given to all the many animals. The first horse was named Gypsy; the first cat, Daniel; first cow, Becky; first dog, Sita. I remember Nancy and Joan Robertson naming a group of chickens. Some interesting names were Marilyn Monroe, showing her beautiful wings; Cleopatra, because of her stately strutting; Cross Beak, named because her upper and lower beaks were crossed and she was rejected by many of the other chickens. But she was by far the most interesting chicken because every morning she came down to the farmhouse to meet the milker of the day and lead him or her back to the barn. Speaking of cows, we have a wonderful picture of Jane while milking, squirting milk into the mouth of Freddy the barn cat. I remember Florence and Else helping a cow give birth in their New Year's Eve gowns.

CELEBRATIONS

There have been many weddings here at the Farm. The first was between me and Don Raiche who met at the Farm—and of course, Nancy and Norm's wedding. For many years, the Farm's gift to the outer community was cooking a four-course meal on Christmas Eve. Sometimes we had 40 or more people—such eating and drinking and singing, and an exchange of gifts by our long time Santa, Bill Smith. The Fourth of July was a celebration, too. We would gather in a circle and sing patriotic songs and we'd enjoy fireworks and games, and roast hot dogs and s'mores.

PLAY

Helen thought we should play, so we had a lot of parties especially at the lake homes of Janet and the Rubins. At one particular party, we were skinny dipping at night while Florence held a sheet on the deck separating the men from the women. All of a sudden we heard, "Don't anyone move. I've lost my glasses," from Walter Gallant. I can't remember if he did find them. At several parties we would lose track of Joanne until someone remembered to look behind the couch where she had fallen asleep.

DANCING

One time we were treated by the performance of a dance club run by Susan Deali on the lawn in front of Tali House. The ladies I remember were Nancy and Joan Hector, Joanne, Kitty and Aphrodite. Another great dance was performed by the same people, plus Maureen, Helen and Deb Baier to the music of the *Lion King* for my eightieth birthday. And of course, we danced at Marcia and Bruce's wedding. Occasionally we used to dance while Bud Witt played the piano until he got tired.

ART

It was a great joy to have Mark Nepo come once every other month to teach us how to appreciate and write poetry. For several years we had a Sunday art club. Each year we set up our artwork. We had an art show each year in the Round House. Some of the most beautiful work was displayed.

Else Hope with Lisa.

Apple Farm Cooks

Nancy Hector Kurilik

It has been a real treat for me to think about and write some stories of our Apple Farm cooks. I realize how individual they have been and I am grateful for their dedication and creativity in bringing food to our table.

This story begins with Else, of course, who gave her intuitive and sensational sense of taste and grace, making our meals special and famous. She brought recipes from her German family, which became regular fare and part of Apple Farm history: kalte Ente (cold duck), Herring Salat and Bienenstich (bee sting) almond cake to name a few.

Later Rose Rubin joined the list of cooks and she brought her Russian-Jewish flavor. Nobody can forget her Russian-style borscht or her "unreknowned" Jewish-style spaghetti sauce.

Martha Echols brought recipes from the convent and all of us novices remembered the gravel pit coffee cake from days at the cottage. She did some cooking for us, but not for long.

I must include Jane in here as an important addition. She did cook more than a bit, but mainly she was a great supervisor, taster and meat carver. She taught me to cut up a chicken as well as carve meat (across the grain to make it more tender). And she was a bartender, famous for the Saturday Night Special, the El Presidente, and our Easter drink the New Orleans gin fizz.

Jean Clampitt cooked for us—mainly, I believe, to help us out and she did so with great dedication and care.

Maureen O'Malley spent quite some time in the kitchen. She had a wonderful attention for detail and her meals were good!

I must add here that in the early days we had animals at the barn: a cow providing us with milk and cream, butter and rich desserts. Why we didn't all get fat is beyond me. We raised pigs and this meant tubs of lard in which to make French fries or anything else that seemed good. Our meat supply included beef, pork and lamb, so we had a great variety of menus.

Jean Harrah was our cook for some time. She loved cooking and was good. She even went to cooking school after she left Apple Farm to become a caterer in Ann Arbor. She catered for the Farm a few times.

Today our ideas about eating have changed. This happened mainly when Charlotte Smith became our cook. Thanks to her she brought in more recipes with fruit, vegetables, pastas and salad to lighten our fare. It was during Charlotte's time that Apple Farm produced a cook book, later a second one. Charlotte was a good cook. She even watched all those cooking shows on TV to improve her craft which was considerable.

Elanor became one of our best cooks. She and Charlotte worked together a lot, sharing their interest in cooking magazines and trying out new recipes. When Charlotte left the kitchen, Elanor became our head chef and remains so to this day.

I spent a lot of time in the kitchen from day one, mostly doing dishes or completing a meal and putting it on the table after the real cook went home. I learned to cook in the beginning from Else and as the years moved on I gathered courage and more skill from all the cooks. I also did a good deal of the cooking.

These stories may not be in chronological order, but close enough. Please forgive me if I have spoken in error or have missed anyone. These are my memories.

The Living Word: Poetry Inspired by Apple Farm

First Time at Apple Farm

KATHY STIFFNEY

I had heard of you for years.
I have known you only a short time.
There is cellular memory stirring.

The china teacups sip me back to my mother's collection
And mind.
The simple kitchen brings my grandmother's hand
Preparing baked beans and buckwheat pancakes.
The barn is once again my childhood dream
Of owning a horse.
I reminisce of times when I, too, was a gardener.

There is call to new.
The woods already commands poetry.
I wait in anticipation the first flare of fall.
The library, Helen's journaling
Transport me back, and beyond,
Different ways of looking at life giving me
Plenty to ponder.
I am touched by fresh souls
Hoping I may touch back.

One thing not yet seen:
An apple.
But I am confident I will
And inside will be the hidden star.

There Are No Rules

JANE BISHOP

There are no rules now.
You who bore me, taught me, raised me,
Mother, Father, friends, lovers,
You are my brothers and sisters now.

All that you taught me to help me in life
Is no longer true, unless I find it so.
Your truths for you, mine for me.

But I, being some part child still,
Grieve for the missing parents to be no more;
Nor to be a parent myself.
No longer even a child of God but co-creator.

This is frightening.
This is glorious.

I am a reluctant miner

DONICE WOOSTER

I came to Apple Farm as a guest in the mid-1980s, and after a long hiatus returned to the Farm when I had an opportunity to take a one-month solitary retreat. I spent that month in the Hut, made a new relationship with the Farm, and have been coming regularly since then. On one stay, the image came to me of inner work as mining, and this poem explores that image.

I am a reluctant miner,
Standing at an open shaft,
Tracks laid down to take me in,
Carts to haul out ore and gold,
Metal, dirt, stones, remains.

My hands find my empty pockets,
Provisions are at my feet.
Overhead, clouds go astray
And shadows play over the timbers
That make and frame the portal.

Quiet lies along my arms
And every cell is tuned.
From deep in the mine, on a breath of air,
A green and unknown scent
And a faint, clear bell for signal.

Emptiness and Grace

Diane DeVaul

I was young when I first
discovered I lacked some
fundamental element others seemed to have.
There was the stomachache
that didn't go away and
the way my mother wouldn't
look at me when the doctor said
nothing was wrong. It was
confusing, I would want to be by myself and
    then
feel empty, lonely, long for
others when I finally was alone.
I was the sitter-in-all-tales
the invisible one. Much later
one day I walked down 2nd Street SE in
    Washington, D.C.,
between my office and a small café and realized I
    had a
hole inside that nothing could fill up no matter how
    hard I tried.
And I tried really hard for a very long time. So
    when
I see this four-day silent retreat
on emptiness I think perfect
I'm going to stare down this emptiness. To my
    surprise
I find that the problem
isn't the emptiness but not
being empty enough. So

I start sorting through my old ideas, rummaging
    through
them like the closet I haven't cleaned
in sixty-eight years. If I clean
out enough maybe here will be
room for grace
for something new.

February 28, 2012

Diane died of colon cancer a little more than a year after she wrote this poem. From 2011 to 2012, she lived at the Farm in Orchard House.

Learning to Speak in the Moon

Ruthann K. Johansen

for Gwendolyn Brooks

In the moon your voice
calls me out
like sun sucking
crocuses from dark mother

Earth, round and
around I turn this
truth that rises beneath
the whited sepulcher

I guard against
breaking, o, open to
rhythms of words
never spoken,

feelings white washed
out of sight, without
sound—o—nly
silence.

Over and over low
your voice washes
black sounds into
translucent language—

you and the moon pulling my
petrified tongue toward

the edge, o,
of water.

Speak, white-woman-to
black-woman, you say;
o, I moan, my sighs
are too high for the hearing.

Babble, you say, like
a brook, water softening,
baptizing the tongue
for truth—one's holy vocation—

lets sounds ripple underground,
unformed in the dark
Earth soil-woman soul;
black woman, you urge

me, white woman, toward
language knit full circle
in my darkness, o,
not of slavery but betrayal.

Speaking black-woman-to-white-woman
you lift me from lying
bondage to shame, o,
breaking pale silence into colorful sound.

Diane

LALLA

On the way to God the difficulties
feel like being ground by a millstone,
like night coming at noon, like
lightning through the clouds.
But don't worry!
What must come, comes.
Face everything with love,
as your mind dissolves in God.

Deep Woods

KATHY STIFFNEY

I have gone deep
Deeper than I would have guessed
Too deep to know what is ahead and where it will go
I have been brave
Following the trail
Choosing at the forks

Would I be so brave
If I were making the trail
My decision where to go and what to do

I have gone deep
Then beyond
A steep descent and a bend
Uneasy fear
An unknown that keeps me frozen
Too deep to know what is ahead
Or where it will go

Choice
Ahead or back?
Ahead?
BACK
Maybe not so brave after all.

Tortoise Prayer (at Apple Farm)

KAREN BRANAN

When you meet a tortoise on the trail
Ancient, leathern, mud-caked,
Entirely aware,
Bow
Give gratitude,
Sit
But do not think to
out-sit,

Lotus position is proper
though not necessary

Lay down your stick
To this god
Of slow things
And remember last night's dream.

Remember also your last thought
Before he lumbered
Into your shadow:

How delicious was the sun
And the languor
Of your gait.

April 2000

Rebeginnings

RUTHANN K. JOHANSEN

Word
threads sent out
invisibly,
tentatively seek
places to weave
mystery
webs to catch the heart,
dumb the tongue,
still the brain before
aha!
Incarnate surprise.

Death II

DIANE DEVAUL

Death hovers in the air.
I try to pin it down
eyes open, but it drifts
hazily away. I can't get the taste of it. I've
given up trying to chase it off. Sometimes
I fantasize taking
death as a lover who
will transport me away.
I read somewhere if you embrace death
you wake to the joy
of life. But like most
things people say, you
can't count on it or maybe
I can't bring myself to actually embrace
death—
the dilemma of the half-lived
life. Instead my brain
calculates or tries the
probability of having three
months, a year, five.

I take my granddaughter
for a walk, still trying to
sense how close death is.
Then I remember summer's
milk weed pods splitting open
seeds parachuting in the wind.
They fly not knowing where
they will land. When the breeze
blows just so I'll be swept away
with no more ability to chart my
course or name the hour.

October 7, 2010

Apple Farm Woods

KATHY STIFFNEY

After buckets of rain
The woods I traipse is drippy, cooled
A lush contrast of black and green
Clean

Some ones have laid the trail
I need not think
Only choose and follow

So much attention to each step
So much beauty missed
Looking down

A sound
My gaze lifts
The deer beyond
The turtle across my path
The fast and pressing
The slow and patient
Living contrast

I Feel at Home

JOANNE HOLDEN

"I feel at home," Helen said at her 90th birthday
    celebration.
She looked around and said, "I feel at
    home."
And so do I.

It's as if she provided a home to come back
    to,
A home for us who were homeless.
As if something has been allowed—
Some vital thing has been allowed which hadn't
    been before,
Some vital thing that was always in us but not
    allowed elsewhere,
And for her to feel at home
Must have meant that we allowed that same thing in
    her,
That we have all allowed this for each other;
A vitality so basic and so simple
As to enable us to feel "at home."

Isn't that wonderful?